THE ULTIMATE
WATER RESOURCES DEPTH EXAM

TABLE OF CONTENTS

WELCOME!!

Welcome to The Ultimate Water Resources Depth Exam! Thank you so much for purchasing this book!

This exam goes over 40 questions and solutions covering the water resources depth exam. This exam is updated to meet the new 2015 specifications. It is designed to have a similar look and feel to the real exam.

The depth exam is typically a much harder exam than the breadth. You should be spending quite a bit of your time in your depth section so that you can score well. Keep in mind though, that if you can crush the morning portion then the afternoon will be much easier on you as they add both scores for your final score. Having said that though, you should be spending 60 to 70% of your time in your depth section.

This test is not endorsed by the NCEES organization. These are problems that my team and I have written to help you succeed in passing the PE exam. I would encourage you to take this timed to see how well you do. Afterwards, you can take note of the areas that you might need to work on. I have spent some time getting all of the information here for you so that it is easy to use. Each problem is labeled so you know what problem and area you are dealing with.

There are multiple ways of taking practice exams – you can work problems like homework, you can take it like the real exam - it's really up to you! I would make sure to do at least one practice exam as if it were the real deal though so you gain that experience.

As always, I value your feedback and any constructive criticism you might have on this exam or anything else we produce to help others pass. You can also get many more resources on the sites we run at www.civilengineeringacademy and www.civilpereviewcourse.com; including step-by-step video practice problems.

I know that with a lot of practice you will become much more proficient at working problems and doing them with less and less assistance. Keep at it and you will be prepared to pass the PE.

I don't need to tell you about the benefits of obtaining your PE license because I'm sure you already know them. You must get it to have a great career in civil engineering (and a lot of other fields!).

As always, I wish you the best of luck!

Sincerely,

Isaac Oakeson, P.E.

(You're going to have that by your name too!)

P.S. Errata for this and any other exam we've made can be found at www.civilengineeringacademy.com/errata. You can join our *free* course on how to prepare, take, and pass the civil PE exam by checking out https://www.civilpereviewcourse.com/freetraining.

LEGAL INFORMATION

Civil Engineering Academy's

The Ultimate Water Resources Depth Exam

Isaac Oakeson, P.E.

Rights and Liability:

If you find errors in this book (I am human of course), or just want to comment on things, then please let me know! I can be reached through the website at www.civilengineeringacademy.com or by email at isaac@civilengineeringacademy.com.

ABOUT THE AUTHOR

Isaac Oakeson, P.E. is a registered professional civil engineer in the great state of Utah. Shortly after passing the PE exam in the Fall of 2012 he started www.civilengineeringacademy.com and www.civilpereviewcourse.com to help future students pass. He has authored and helped author various exams with his entire goal of providing the best resources for engineers to study and pass the PE.

CIVIL – WATER RESOURCES and ENVIRONMENTAL DEPTH EXAM SPECIFICATIONS

I. Analysis and Design (4)

A. Mass balance

B. Hydraulic loading

C. Solids loading (e.g., sediment loading, sludge)

D. Hydraulic flow measurement

II. Hydraulics–Closed Conduit (5)

A. Energy and/or continuity equation (e.g., Bernoulli, momentum equation)

B. Pressure conduit (e.g., single pipe, force mains, Hazen-Williams, Darcy-Weisbach, major and minor losses)

C. Pump application and analysis, including wet wells, lift stations, and cavitation

D. Pipe network analysis (e.g., series, parallel, and loop networks)

III. Hydraulics–Open Channel (5)

A. Open-channel flow

B. Hydraulic energy dissipation

C. Stormwater collection and drainage (e.g., culvert, stormwater inlets, gutter flow, street flow, storm sewer pipes)

D. Sub- and supercritical flow

IV. Hydrology (7)

A. Storm characteristics (e.g., storm frequency, rainfall measurement, and distribution)

B. Runoff analysis (e.g., Rational and SCS/NRCS methods)

C. Hydrograph development and applications, including synthetic hydrographs

D. Rainfall intensity, duration, and frequency

E. Time of concentration

F. Rainfall and stream gauging stations

G. Depletions (e.g., evaporation, detention, percolation, and diversions)

H. Stormwater management (e.g., detention ponds, retention ponds, infiltration systems, and swales)

V. Groundwater and Wells (3)

A. Aquifers

B. Groundwater flow

C. Well analysis–steady state

VI. Wastewater Collection and Treatment (6)

A. Wastewater collection systems (e.g., lift stations, sewer networks, infiltration, inflow, smoke testing, maintenance, and odor control)

B. Wastewater treatment processes

C. Wastewater flow rates

D. Preliminary treatment

E. Primary treatment

F. Secondary treatment (e.g., physical, chemical, and biological processes)

G. Nitrification/denitrification

H. Phosphorus removal

I. Solids treatment, handling, and disposal

J. Digestion

K. Disinfection

L. Advanced treatment (e.g., physical, chemical, and biological processes)

VII. Water Quality (3)

A. Stream degradation

B. Oxygen dynamics

C. Total maximum daily load (TMDL) (e.g., nutrient contamination, DO, load allocation)

D. Biological contaminants

E. Chemical contaminants, including bioaccumulation

VIII. Drinking Water Distribution and Treatment (6)

A. Drinking water distribution systems

B. Drinking water treatment processes

C. Demands

D. Storage

E. Sedimentation

F. Taste and odor control

G. Rapid mixing (e.g., coagulation)

H. Flocculation

I. Filtration

J. Disinfection, including disinfection byproducts

K. Hardness and softening

IX. Engineering Economics Analysis (1)

A. Economic analysis (e.g., present worth, lifecycle costs, comparison of alternatives)

START TEST

1. In the figure shown below, a vertical pipe is discharging water from an elevated tank into the atmosphere. Determine the diameter of the pipe that can produce a discharge of 10.2 ft³/s considering a 0.15% velocity head loss per feet length of the pipe.

a) 2.4 in
b) 5.5 in
c) 6 in
d) 7 in

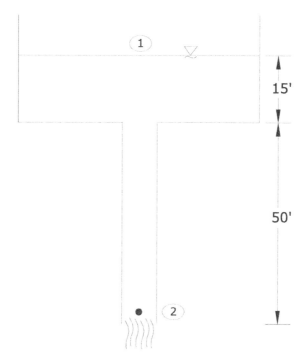

2. The velocity of the water before a pump is 26 ft/s with 13 psi of pressure. It has a head of 16 ft. The pressure at the discharge side of the pump is 22 psi. Assuming that the elevation of the pipes before and after the pump are the same, and neglecting head loss, determine the discharge after the pump if the diameter of the pipe is 8 in.

a) 6.7 ft³/s
b) 7.7 ft³/s
c) 8.7 ft³/s
d) 9.7 ft³/s

3. A 300-ft long pipe, 5 inch in diameter, carries a liquid having a kinematic viscosity of 2 x 10⁻⁴ ft²/s. If the flow rate is 0.035 ft³/s, determine the head loss.

a) 1.1 in
b) 1.5 in
c) 2.6 in
d) 3.2 in

4. A fluid is flowing in a 4-in diameter pipe. The frictional stress between the fluid and the pipewall is 0.4 lbf/ft². Calculate the most nearly head loss due to friction if the specific weight of fluid is 50 lbf/ft³ and the length of the pipe is 50 ft.

Hint: Use this formula to find shear stress of the wall of pipe

$$\tau_o = \frac{fV^2\rho}{8g}$$

a) 2 ft
b) 3 ft
c) 4 ft
d) 5 ft

5. Which of the following factors explains why the energy gradient is always parallel to the hydraulic gradient?

a) Head
b) Discharge
c) Area
d) None of the above

6. A closed conduit with a 8-in diameter is connected to a 10-in pipe. The velocity of the first pipe is 8 ft/s. Determine the velocity of the second pipe.

a) 3 ft/s
b) 5 ft/s
c) 8 ft/s
d) 10 ft/s

7. The bottom of a canal has a width of 10 ft and the side slopes are 2 horizontal to 1 vertical. If the roughness coefficient is 0.022 and the slope of the energy gradient is 0.23%, find the discharge when the water flows at 3-ft deep.

a) 190 ft³/s
b) 250 ft³/s
c) 320 ft³/s
d) 350 ft³/s

8. In a 13 ft wide rectangular channel, the water flowing at a depth of 1.5 ft jumps to a depth of 5 ft. Determine the most nearly discharge flowing in the channel.

a) 365 ft³/s
b) 490 ft³/s
c) 845 ft³/s
d) 1820 ft³/s

9. The critical depth of a trapezoidal channel is 3 ft. The channel has a bottom width of 15 ft with side slope upward at an angle of 45°. Determine the flow at a critical flow condition.

a) 350 cfs
b) 405 cfs
c) 491 cfs
d) 552 cfs

10. A 50-ft concrete pipe culvert has a diameter of 5 ft discharges water as shown in the figure. Estimate its probable capacity if the head, h is 6 ft and the coefficient of discharge $C_d = 0.73$.

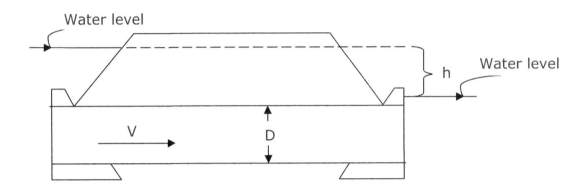

a) 171 cfs
b) 205 cfs
c) 281 cfs
d) 304 cfs

11. A storm drain tunnel is shown in the figure. During a heavy storm the water surface reaches 6 ft above the semi-circular section. If the Manning's coefficient of roughness is 0.02 and the slope is 0.0006, determine the velocity of the flow.

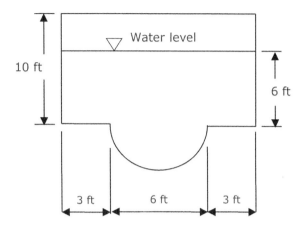

a) 0.6 ft/s
b) 1.8 ft/s
c) 2.7 ft/s
d) 3.9 ft/s

12. What term represents the design flood for a particular project as determined by a contract?

a) Probably maximum flood (PMF)
b) Design basis flood (DBF)
c) Standard project flood (SBF)
d) None of the above

CIVIL
ENGINEERING
ACADEMY

13. In a 25-yr rainfall event, the intensity of the rain of a 75-acre industrial park is 3 in/h. Using the rational method, determine the runoff rate of an industrial park with a C factor of 0.75.

a) 135 ft³/s
b) 145 ft³/s
c) 150 ft³/s
d) 170 ft³/s

14. From the Intensity-Duration-Frequency Curve shown in the figure, determine the rainfall depth for a 7-minute rainfall event considering a 10-year return period.

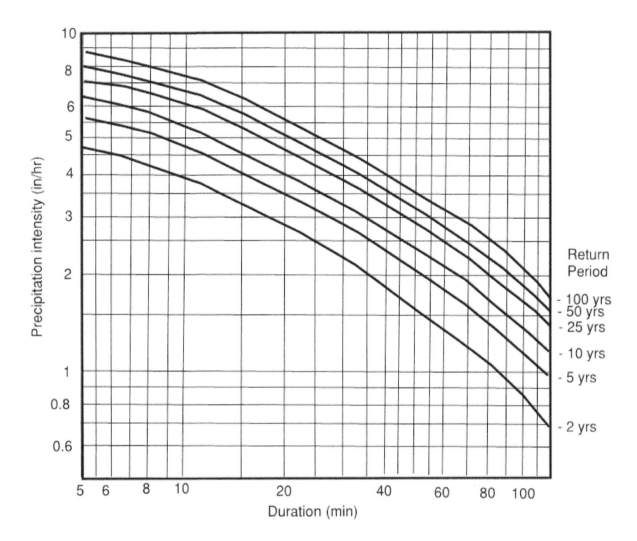

a) 42 inches
b) 0.7 inch
c) 6 inches
d) 0.4 inch

15. In a certain area, the amount of precipitation during a three-hour rainfall event is 75 inches with a runoff of 3 inches. Determine the infiltration rate.

a) 24 in/hr
b) 27 in/hr
c) 15 in/hr
d) 31 in/hr

16. The precipitation of a certain place is 20 inches with a surface runoff of 5 inches, subsurface outflow of 4 inches, and evapotranspiration of 1.5 inches. Determine the change in moisture storage.

a) 7.2 in
b) 8.4 in
c) 9.0 in
d) 9.5 in

CIVIL
ENGINEERING
ACADEMY

17. A certain typhoon has an average rainfall of 1.5 inch in a four-hour duration over an area of 1.1×10^8 ft^2. If the fraction of precipitation is 30%, neglecting base flow, what is the volume of the runoff?

a) 4×10^6 ft^3
b) 1.2×10^7 ft^3
c) 4×10^7 ft^3
d) 1.7×10^8 ft^3

18. In a watershed, station A is located 58,682 ft away from the outlet. If the average slope is 0.0006, determine the time of concentration using Kirpich equation:

$$t_c = 0.0078 L^{0.77} S^{-0.385}$$

a) 547 min
b) 637 min
c) 658 min
d) 741 min

19. Calculate the specific discharge of an aquifer having a hydraulic conductivity of 100 ft/day and an effective porosity of 25%. The hydraulic gradient is 0.0004.

a) 4.6 x 10^{-7} ft/s
b) 1.15 x 10^{-7} ft/s
c) 1.85 x 10^{-8} ft/s
d) 1.00 x 10^{-8} ft/s

20. A sanitary sewer has a length of 260 ft and a pipe with a diameter of 3 ft. The inlet elevation of the sewer is 4 ft higher than the outlet elevation. Assume that the Manning roughness coefficient is 0.01 with a constant with depth of flow. Determine the sewer capacity/discharge during heavy rainfalls if the sewer is full of water flow with no surcharge.

a)   93 ft³/s
b)   100 ft³/s
c)   108 ft³/s
d)   135 ft³/s

21. In an unconfined aquifer, two observation wells at 300 ft apart were monitored. At the first & second well, the water stands 26 ft & 20 ft above the bottom, respectively. If the hydraulic conductivity of the aquifer is 6.7×10^{-4} in/s, what is its discharge per 50-ft wide strip?

a)   70 ft^3/day
b)   80 ft^3/day
c)   110 ft^3/day
d)   150 ft^3/day

22. A well is pumped in an unconfined aquifer. In an observation well at 150 ft away from the pumped well, the drawdown is 13 ft. Another observation well is located 600 ft away from the pumped well and has an observed drawdown of 2.45 ft. The initial depth of the water table is at 45 ft above the bedrock (non-aquifer layer). If the coefficient of permeability is 0.00788 ft/s, determine the discharge of the well.

a)   5 ft³/s
b)   8 ft³/s
c)   9 ft³/s
d)   14 ft³/s

23. A certain city has an average wastewater flow rate of 50,500,000 gpd. If the peaking factor is 2.4, what is the closest peak wastewater flow rate?

a) 21,000,000 gpd
b) 210,000,000 gpd
c) 120,000,000 gpd
d) 12,000,000 gpd

24. What is the purpose of secondary treatment in wastewater treatment plants, and what are the most common types of secondary treatment processes used?

a) To remove dissolved and suspended inorganic matter, and the most common types of secondary treatment processes used are sedimentation and filtration

b) To remove dissolved and suspended organic matter, and the most common types of secondary treatment processes used are sedimentation and disinfection

c) To remove dissolved and suspended organic matter, and the most common types of secondary treatment processes used are activated sludge, trickling filters, and rotating biological contactors

d) To remove dissolved and suspended inorganic matter, and the most common types of secondary treatment processes used are activated sludge, trickling filters, and disinfection

25. The design average flow of a trickling filter plant effluent is 2.75 MGD. If its recommended dosage is 10 mg/L, estimate the monthly supply of the liquid chlorine for the plant. (Hint: For application of chlorine of more than 150 lb/day, one-ton (short) containers are employed.)

a) 1 container
b) 2 containers
c) 3 containers
d) 4 containers

26. An influent with a nitrate-N of 20 mg/L, nitrite-N of 0.45 mg/L and DO of 2.0 mg/L undergoes a complete denitrification process. Calculate the methanol dosage requirement.

a) 45.1 mg/L
b) 51.8 mg/L
c) 65.2 mg/L
d) 98.7 mg/L

27. A residual (sludge) initially contains 0.8% (P_1) of solids and thickened to 5% (P_2). If the final volume of the thickened sludge is 18,000 ft³, determine its initial volume.

a)   57,500 ft³
b)   72,500 ft³
c)   112,500 ft³
d)   132,500 ft³

28. Which of the following statements is false?

a) A secondary treatment is an effective way of removing non-biodegradable organics and heavy metals.
b) The purpose of a primary treatment is to remove suspended solids and floating material.
c) Secondary treatment has the ability to remove about 85% of BOD_5 and suspended matter.
d) Secondary treatment processes are intended to remove the soluble and colloidal organics.

29. A wastewater underwent a biochemical test. During sampling, the dissolved oxygen of the diluted sample and seeded control were 7.86 mg/L and 8.30 mg/L, respectively. After five days, the dissolved oxygen of the diluted sample and seeded control were 2.5 mg/L and 8.0 mg/L, respectively. One mL of waste sample was added to dillution water to 20 mL. Determine the BOD_5.

a) 101 mg/L
b) 105 mg/L
c) 110 mg/L
d) 207 mg/L

30. What is the definition of chemical oxygen demand (COD) in wastewater treatment, and which of the following is the primary factor affecting the COD test results?

a) COD is a measure of the total organic matter in wastewater, and the primary factor affecting the COD test results is the concentration of suspended solids

b) COD is a measure of the total inorganic matter in wastewater, and the primary factor affecting the COD test results is the pH of the sample

c) COD is a measure of the total organic matter in wastewater, and the primary factor affecting the COD test results is the presence of chloride ions

d) COD is a measure of the total organic matter in wastewater, and the primary factor affecting the COD test results is the presence of reducing agents

31. The calculation of numerical estimates of risk for each substance through each route of exposure, using the dose-response information as the exposure estimates is called:

a) Hazard identification
b) Dose-response evaluation
c) Exposure assessment
d) Risk characterization

32. Which of the following indicator bacteria are used in standards for drinking-water and natural waters?

a) Total Coliform and Fecal Streptococcus
b) Total Coliform and Fecal Coliform
c) Fecal Coliform and Fecal Streptococcus
d) None of the above

33. Which of the following things is a measure of the amount of organic matter oxidized by a strong chemical oxidant?

a) TSS
b) COD
c) BOD
d) DO

34. In a certain townhouse, flow reduction devices were installed at the faucet, shower head, washing machine, and toilet. The table shows the effect of the flow reduction devices. Determine the percentage reduction in the flow of water.

a) 39.5%
b) 83%
c) 20.8%
d) 28.3%

Items	Flow in liters/person/day	
	Without reduction devices	With reduction devices
1. Faucet	65	55
2. Shower head	58	35
3. Washing machine	45	30
4. Toilet	125	90

35. A water treatment plant is designing a coagulation and flocculation unit for a water treatment process. The unit is required to have a mean velocity gradient (G) of at least 45/sec to ensure effective coagulation and flocculation. The fluid being treated has a dynamic viscosity (μ) of 0.01 lbf-sec/ft^2 and a volume (V) of 5000 gal. What is the minimum power (P) required for the unit to achieve the desired gradient velocity?

a) 2.50 hp
b) 20.00 hp
c) 25.00 hp
d) 250.00 hp

36. Determine the dimension (W x L) of a sedimentation basin which is to be designed to remove 100% of all particles with a settling velocity of 0.012 in/s for flow discharge of 282 ft³/min. The length of the basin must be such that it is three times its width.

a)   40 ft x 120 ft
b)   50 ft x 150 ft
c)   60 ft x 180 ft
d)   70 ft x 210 ft

37. A rapid filter plant is composed of 15 units. Each filter unit has a width of 16 ft and a length of 32 ft. Its medium is sand with an effective size of 0.02 in and a uniformity coefficient of 1.4. If the volume of the treated water produced per day is 4 millions ft^3, determine the nominal filtration rate.

a) 520 ft/day
b) 825 ft/day
c) 1210 ft/day
d) 1350 ft/day

38. From the graph shown below, determine the chlorine dosage to achieve the breakpoint in the chlorine demand curve.

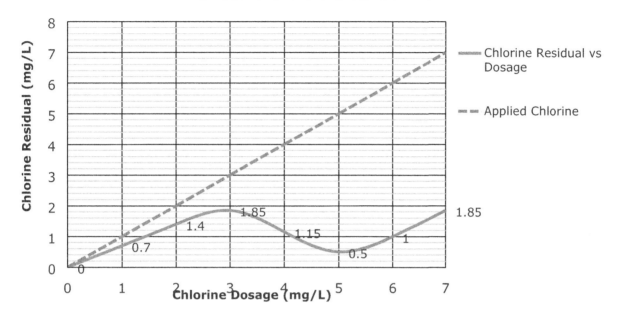

a) 0.5 mg/L
b) 1.85 mg/L
c) 3 mg/L
d) 5 mg/L

39. Which of the following is the process of removal of calcium, magnesium, and certain other metal cations in hard water.

a) Desalination
b) Water softening
c) Water disinfection
d) Distillation

40. In an aeration tank, two 5-hp motors run 24 hours per day. One motor, an older model, has an efficiency of 85% while the new model has an efficiency of 92%. If the electricity cost is $0.02 per kW-h, determine the monthly power cost.

a) $97.50
b) $121.60
c) $154.85
d) $302.21

PROBLEM SOLUTIONS

CIVIL
ENGINEERING
ACADEMY

Energy and/or Continuity Equation (Bernoulli's Theorem)

Problem 1 Solution:

Bernoulli's Energy Equation 1 to 2: datum 2

$$\frac{P_1}{\gamma} + \frac{V_1^2}{2g} + Z_1 = \frac{P_2}{\gamma} + \frac{V_2^2}{2g} + Z_2 + h_{f_{1-2}}$$

Since the tank is open, the pressure at point 1 is atmospheric, thus pressure head at point 1 is zero.

At the top of the tank, the water is still; thus velocity = 0

At point 2, the water is released at the atmosphere. Pressure head at point 2 is zero.

At point 2, elevation head Z_2 is zero since it is the datum.

$$0 + 0 + 65 = 0 + \frac{V_2^2}{2g} + 0 + 0.015 \times 50 \times \frac{V_2^2}{2g}$$

$$65 = (1 + 0.75)\frac{V_2^2}{2g}$$

$$65 = \frac{1.75V_2^2}{2g}$$

$$V_2 = \sqrt{\frac{65 \times 2(32.2)}{1.75}} = 48.91 \text{ ft/s}$$

$$Q = AV$$

$$A = \frac{10.2 \text{ ft}^3/s}{48.91 \text{ ft/s}} = 0.209 \text{ ft}^2$$

$$A = \frac{\pi d^2}{4}$$

$$d = \sqrt{\frac{4A}{\pi}} = \sqrt{\frac{4 \times 0.209}{\pi}} = 0.5 \text{ ft} = 6 \text{ in}$$

Reference: PERH 1.2 Section 6.2.1.2 Energy Equation

(Answer C)

Pump Application and Analysis

Problem 2 Solution:

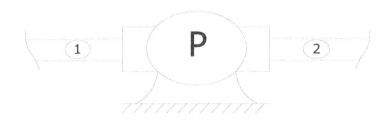

$$\frac{V_1^2}{2g} + \frac{P_1}{\gamma} + Z_1 + H.A. = \frac{V_2^2}{2g} + \frac{P_2}{\gamma} + Z_2 + H.L.$$

$$\frac{26^2}{2(32.2)} + \frac{13(144)}{62.4} + 0 + 16 = \frac{V_2^2}{2(32.2)} + \frac{22(144)}{62.4} + 0 + 0$$

$$V_2 = 19.2 \text{ ft/s}$$

$$Q = AV = \frac{\pi \left(\frac{8}{12}\right)^2}{4} \times 19.2 = 6.7 \text{ ft}^3/\text{s}$$

Reference: PERH 1.2 Section 6.2.1.2 Energy Equation

(Answer A)

Flow Measurement (Closed Conduit)

Problem 3 Solution:

To find the head loss, determine first if the flow inside the pipe is laminar or turbulent by computing the Reynold's number.

$$\text{Re} = \frac{DV}{v}$$

Re = Reynold's number, if less the 2000 means the flow is laminar

D = diameter of pipe in ft

V = average velocity in ft/s

v = kinematic viscosity in ft^2/s

$$Q = AV \rightarrow V = \frac{0.035 \text{ ft}^3/\text{s}}{\frac{\pi}{4} \times \left(\frac{5 \text{ in}}{12 \text{ in/ft}}\right)^2} = 0.257 \text{ ft/s}$$

Therefore, $\text{Re} = \dfrac{DV}{v} = \dfrac{\dfrac{5 \text{ in}}{12 \text{ in/ft}} \times 0.257 \text{ ft/s}}{2 \times 10^{-4} \text{ ft}^2/\text{s}} = 535 < 2000$ (Laminar flow)

Use equation $f = \dfrac{64}{\text{Re}} = \dfrac{64}{535} = 0.12$

To calculate the head loss, use equation:

$$h_f = f \frac{L}{D} \frac{V^2}{2g} = 0.12 \times \frac{300 \text{ ft}}{\left(\dfrac{5 \text{ in}}{12 \text{ in/ft}}\right)} \times \frac{(0.257 \text{ ft/s})^2}{2 \times 32.2 \text{ ft}^2/\text{s}} = 0.088 \text{ ft} = 1.1 \text{ in}$$

Reference: PERH 1.2 Section 6.2.2.2 Reynolds Number-Circular Pipes & Section 6.2.3.1 Head Loss Due To Flow (Darcy-Weisbach)

(Answer A)

Friction and Minor Losses

Problem 4 Solution:

Shear stress of the wall of pipe $\tau_o = \dfrac{fV^2 \rho}{8g}$

Where: τ_o = shear stress in lbf/ft²

f = friction factor

h_f = head loss in ft

ρ = specific weight in lbf/ft³

Using the shear stress equation and substituting the values:

$$0.4 = \frac{fV^2 \times 50}{8 \times 32.2}$$
$$fV^2 = 2.0608$$

Calculating the head loss:

$$h_f = \frac{fV^2 \times L}{D2g} = \frac{2.0608 \times 50}{\left(\dfrac{4}{12}\right) \times 2 \times 32.2} = 3.84 \text{ ft}$$

Reference: PERH 1.2 Section 6.2.2.2 Reynolds Number-Circular Pipes & Section 6.2.3.1 Head Loss Due To Flow (Darcy-Weisbach)

(Answer C)

Hydraulic Grade Line & Energy Line

Problem 5 Solution:

They velocity head is the reason why the energy grade line and the hydraulic grade line are always parallel. The energy grade line is all three terms of the energy equation and is always above the hydraulic grade line. The hydraulic grade line is only the pressure head and the elevation head. It does not include the velocity head. The difference between the two lines is the velocity head ($v^2/2g$).

Reference: PERH 1.2 Section 6.2.1.4 Hydraulic Gradient (Grade Line) & Section 6.2.1.5 Energy Line (Bernoulli Equation)

(Answer D)

Pipe Network Analysis (Pipes in Series)

Problem 6 Solution:

The two pipes should have the same discharge.

$$Q_1 = Q_2$$
$$A_1 V_1 = A_2 V_2$$
$$V_2 = \frac{A_1 V_1}{A_2}$$
$$V_2 = \frac{\left(\dfrac{\pi}{4} \times \left(\dfrac{8 \text{ in}}{12 \text{ in/ft}}\right)^2\right) \times 8 \text{ ft/s}}{\dfrac{\pi}{4} \times \left(\dfrac{10 \text{ in}}{12 \text{ in/ft}}\right)^2}$$
$$V_2 = 5.12 \text{ ft/s}$$

Reference: PERH 1.2 Section 6.2.1.1 Continuity Equation or Section 6.3.10.1 Network Flow Continuity

(Answer B)

Manning's Equation

Problem 7 Solution:

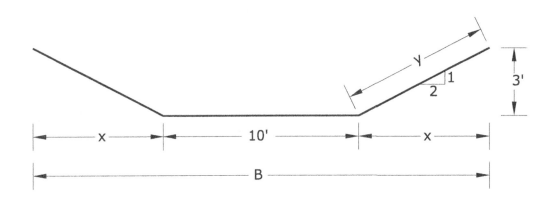

$$\frac{x}{3} = \frac{2}{1}$$
$$x = 6 \text{ ft}$$

$$B = 2x + 10 = 2 \times 6 + 10 = 22 \text{ ft}$$

$$A = \frac{1}{2} \times (10 + 22) \times 3 = 48 \text{ ft}^2$$

$$P = 10 + 2y = 10 + 2 \times \sqrt{6^2 + 3^2} = 23.4 \text{ ft}$$

$$R = \frac{A}{P} = \frac{48}{23.4} = 2.05 \text{ ft}$$

$$Q = \frac{1.486}{n} AR^{\frac{2}{3}} S^{\frac{1}{2}}$$
$$Q = \frac{1.486}{0.022} \times 48 \times 2.05^{\frac{2}{3}} \times 0.0023^{\frac{1}{2}}$$
$$Q = 251 \text{ ft}^3/s$$

Reference: PERH 1.2 Section 6.4.5.1 Manning's Equation

(Answer B)

Energy Dissipation (Hydraulic Jump)

Problem 8 Solution:

Equation of Hydraulic Jump:

$$v_1^2 = \left(\frac{gy_2}{2y_1}\right)(y_1 + y_2)$$

$$= \left(\frac{32.2 \times 5}{2 \times 1.5}\right)(1.5 + 5)$$

$$= 348.8$$

$$v_1 = \sqrt{348.8} = 18.68 \text{ ft/s}$$

$$A_1 = by_1 = 13 \times 1.5 = 19.5 \text{ ft}^2$$

$$Q = A_1 v_1 = 19.5 \times 18.68 = 364.2 \text{ ft}^3/\text{s}$$

Reference: PERH 1.2 Section 6.4.8 Rapidly Varied Flow and Hydraulic Jump

(Answer A)

Critical Flow

Problem 9 Solution:

Using the formula at critical stage:

$$\frac{Q^2 T_c}{g A_c{}^3} = 1$$

Where:

Q = discharge

A_c = area of the channel at critical depth

T_c = width of the channel at the water surface at critical condition

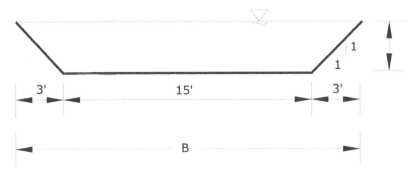

$$T_c = 15' + (2 \times 3') = 21'$$

$$A_c = \frac{(15' + 21')}{2} \times 3' = 54 \text{ ft}^2$$

$$Q^2 = \frac{1 \times \left(32.2 \ \frac{\text{ft}}{\text{s}^2}\right) \times \left(54 \ \text{ft}^2\right)^3}{21 \ \text{ft}} \rightarrow Q = 491.37 \ \text{ft}^3/\text{s}$$

Quick & Simple Approach:

$$Q_c = \left(\frac{A^3 g}{T}\right)^{1/2} = \left(\frac{(54^3)(32.2)}{21}\right)^{1/2} = 491.37 \ \text{ft}^3/\text{s}$$

Reference: PERH 1.2 Section 6.4.3.2 Critical Depth

(Answer C)

Culvert Design

Problem 10 Solution:

$$Q = C_d A \sqrt{2gh}$$

Where: Q = discharge; C_d = coefficient of discharge; A = area; h = difference between headwater and tailwater

Solving for the area, use the Area of the circle using the given diameter of the culvert equal to 5 ft.

$$A = \frac{\pi D^2}{4}$$
$$A = \frac{\pi \times 5^2}{4}$$
$$A = 19.63 \text{ ft}^2$$

Solving for the discharge:

$$Q = C_d A \sqrt{2gh}$$
$$= 0.73 \times 19.63 \times \sqrt{2 \times 32.2 \times 6}$$
$$= 281.68 \text{ cfs}$$

Reference: PERH 1.2 Section 6.4.10.1 Classification of Culvert Flow (USGS Method)

(Answer C)

Flow Measurement - Uniform Flow

Problem 11 Solution:

The velocity of the flow is:

$$V = \frac{1.486}{n} R^{\frac{2}{3}} S^{\frac{1}{2}}$$

Where:

V = velocity

R = hydraulic radius = area/wetted perimeter

S = slope

Solving for the hydraulic radius, the area and the wetted perimeter must be solved first.

Area, A (the area of the semi circle and the area of the rectangle filled with water):

$$A = 12 \times 6 + \frac{1}{2} \times \left(\frac{\pi}{4} \times 6^2 \right) = 86.14 \text{ ft}^2$$

$$P = 2 \times 6 + 2 \times 3 + \frac{1}{2} \times \pi \times 6 = 27.42 \text{ ft}$$

$$R = \frac{A}{P} = \frac{86.14 \text{ ft}^2}{27.4 \text{ ft}} = 3.14 \text{ ft}$$

Therefore:

$$V = \frac{1.486}{0.02} \times 3.14^{\frac{2}{3}} \times 0.0006^{\frac{1}{2}} = 3.9 \text{ ft/s}$$

Reference: PERH 1.2 Section 6.4.5.1 Manning's Equation

(Answer D)

Floodplain/Floodway

Problem 12 Solution:

PMF is a hypothetical flood that can be expected to occur as a result of the most severe combination of meteorological and hydrological conditions possible.

DBF is the flood that is adopted as the basis for the design of a particular project and is determined from economic considerations, or it is specified as part of a contract.

SPF is a flood that can be selected from the most severe combinations of meteorological and hydrological conditions in a particular region, excluding rare combinations. SPF volumes are usually 40-60% of PMF volumes.

The correct answer here is B – DBF.

Reference: FEMA 480 NFIP Floodplain Management Requirements

(Answer B)

Hydrology (Runoff Analysis Including Rational Method)

Problem 13 Solution:

Given:

Area of the drainage basin, A = 75 ac

Precipitation (25-year return period) = 3 in/hr

Find:

Runoff rate if $C = 0.75$

Computations:

Runoff rate, Q

$Q = C I A$

$A = 75$ ac x 43,560 ft^2/ac = 3,267,000 ft^2

$I = 3$ in/hr x 0.083 ft/in x 1hr/3600s = 6.92 x 10^{-5} ft/s

$C = 0.75$

$Q = 0.75$ x 6.92 x 10^{-5} ft/s x 3,267,000 ft^2

$Q = 169.56$ ft^3/s $\approx$ 170 ft^3/s

The runoff rate is approximately 170 ft^3/s.

Reference: PERH 1.2 Section 6.5.2 Runoff Analysis

(Answer D)

Hydrology (Intensity-Duration-Frequency)

Problem 14 Solution:

To solve for the value P, use equation:

$$i = \frac{P}{T_d}$$

Where: i = average intensity

P = rainfall depth

T_d = duration

(from the IDF curve, i = 6 in/hr)

T_d = 7 min = 0.1167 hr

$P = iT_d = 6 \times 0.1167 = 0.7$ in

Reference: PERH 1.2 Section 6.5.6.4 National Weather Service IDF Curve Creation

(Answer B)

Possible answers:

a.) If T_d is not converted into hour, $P = 7 \times 6 = 42$ in
b.) 0.7 (correct answer)
c.) If the student fails to understand the equation, he might answer the intensity instead (6 in)
d.) 0.4 – this value is just to confuse the student

Depletion (Infiltration)

Problem 15 Solution:

$$\text{Inflitration Rate} = \frac{\text{precipitation - runoff}}{\text{duration of rainfall in hours}}$$

$$\text{Inflitration Rate} = \frac{75-3}{3} = 24 \text{ in/hr}$$

Reference: PERH 1.2 Section 6.5.8.1 Surface Water System Hydrologic Budget

(Answer A)

Depletion (Change in moisture Storage)

Problem 16 Solution:

Change in moisture storage = precipitation – surface runoff – subsurface outflow - evapotranspiration

Given:

Precipitation = 20 inches

Surface runoff = 5 inches

Subsurface outflow = 4 inches

Evapotranspiration = 1.5 inches

Change in moisture storage = 20 – 5 – 4 – 1.5 = 9.5 in

Reference: PERH 1.2 Section 6.5.8.1 Surface Water System Hydrologic Budget

(Answer D)

Precipitation, Runoff, Rainfall

Problem 17 Solution:

Note: the base flow is neglected

$$\text{Volume of rainfall} = \left(\frac{1.5 \text{ in}}{12 \text{ in/ft}} \right) \times 1.1 \times 10^8 \text{ ft}^2 = 0.1375 \times 10^8 \text{ ft}^3$$

$$\text{Fraction of precipitation} = \frac{\text{volume of runoff}}{\text{volume of rainfall}} \times 100$$

$$\text{Volume of runoff} = \frac{\text{fraction of precipitation} \times \text{volume of rainfall}}{100}$$

$$= \frac{30}{100} \times 0.1375 \times 10^8 \text{ ft}^2 = 4.125 \times 10^6 \text{ ft}^3$$

Reference: PERH 1.2 Section 6.5.8.1 Surface Water System Hydrologic Budget

(Answer A)

Time of Concentration

Problem 18 Solution:

$$t_c = 0.0078 L^{0.77} S^{-0.385}$$

Where:

t_c = time of concentration (min)

L = length of the channel from the headwater to the outlet (ft)

S = average slope (ft/ft)

$$t_c = 0.0078 \times 58682^{0.77} \times 0.0006^{-0.385} = 637.2 \approx 637 \text{ min}$$

Reference: PERH 1.2 Section 6.5.4 Time of Concentration

(Answer B)

Groundwater and Well Fields -Darcy's Law

Problem 19 Solution:

Given:

Hydraulic conductivity, K = 100 ft/day

Hydraulic gradient, $\frac{dh}{dl} = 0.0004$

Effective porosity, $\eta_e = 0.25$

Find: specific discharge, q

Specific discharge also known as Darcy velocity

Using the equation: $q = -K\frac{dh}{dl}$

$q = -100 \times 0.0004 = -0.04 \text{ ft/day} = \frac{0.04}{1 \times 24 \times 3600} = 4.6 \times 10^{-7}$ ft/s

Reference: PERH 1.2 Section 6.6.2.1 Darcy's Law

(**Answer A**)

Possible Answers:

a.) 4.6×10^{-7} ft/s ------ correct answer

b.) 1.15×10^{-7} ft/s ----- $(100 \times 0.0004 \times 0.25 / (24 \times 3600))$– The correct answer is multiplied by the porosity; this is to confuse the student since porosity is given

c.) 1.85×10^{-6} ft/s --- $(100 \times 0.0004 / 0.25 / (24 \times 3600))$– Still porosity is added in the solution to confuse the use of this parameter

d.) 1.0×10^{-6} ft/s ----$(0.0004 \times 0.25 / 100)$– This answer has no basis at all. In case the student just play with the numbers, he may happen to get this value

Manning's Equation

Problem 20 Solution:

Find the slope of the sewer:

$$S = \frac{Z_{inlet} - Z_{outlet}}{L} = \frac{4}{260} = 0.01538$$

According to the assumption given in the question, the sewer is full of water flow during heavy rainfall. Therefore, it can be assumed that the perimeter is equal to the pipe perimeter P.

Find the hydraulic radius:

$$R = \frac{A}{P} = \frac{\frac{\pi}{4} \times 3^2}{\pi \times 3} = 0.75 \text{ ft}$$

Using Manning's equation, find the flow velocity:

$$v = \frac{1.486}{n} R^{\frac{2}{3}} S^{\frac{1}{2}}$$
$$= \frac{1.486}{0.01} \times 0.75^{\frac{2}{3}} \times 0.01538^{\frac{1}{2}}$$
$$= 15.21 \text{ ft/s}$$

After obtaining flow velocity, the sewer capacity can be calculated:

$$Q = AV = \left(\frac{\pi}{4} \times 3^2 \right) \times 15.21 = 107.5 \text{ cfs}$$

Reference: PERH 1.2 Section 6.4.5.1 Manning's Equation

(Answer C)

Aquifer

Problem 21 Solution:

Given:

Hydraulic conductivity, $K = 6.7 \times 10^{-4}$ in/s
Flow length, $L = 300$ ft
Head at the origin, $h_1 = 26$ ft
Head at L, $h_2 = 20$ ft

Find:

The discharge per 50-ft wide strip of the aquifer in ft³/day, Q

$$Q = q \times b$$

$$q = \frac{1}{2} K \left(\frac{h_1^2 - h_2^2}{L} \right)$$

Where:

q is the flow per unit width (ft²/day)

K is the hydraulic conductivity

h_1 is the head at the origin (ft)

h_2 is the head at L (ft)

L is the flow length (ft)

See next page to see how q equation is derived

Converting the value of K

$$K = \left(6.7 \times 10^{-4} \text{ in/s}\right)(1 \text{ ft/12 in})(3600 \text{ s/hr})(24 \text{ hr/day}) = 4.824 \text{ ft/day}$$

$$q = \frac{1}{2} \times 4.824 \, \frac{\text{ft}}{\text{day}} \times \left(\frac{(26 \text{ ft})^2 - (20 \text{ ft})^2}{300 \text{ ft}} \right) = 2.22 \, \frac{\text{ft}^2}{\text{day}}$$

$$Q = q \times b = 2.22 \, \frac{\text{ft}^2}{\text{day}} \times 50 \text{ ft} = 111 \text{ ft}^3/\text{day}$$

How to derive the equation q:

An analytical solution to the flow is obtained by using Darcy equation to express the velocity, v, at any point, x, with a corresponding hydraulic gradient $\frac{dh}{dx}$, as:

$$v = -K\frac{dh}{dx}$$

Unit discharge, q is calculated to be:

$$q = -Kh\frac{dh}{dx}$$

Considering the origin of the coordinate x at location A where the hydraulic head is h_A and knowing the hydraulic head h_B at a location B, situated at a distance L from A, let's integrate the above differential equation as:

$$\int_0^L qdx = -K\int_{h_A}^{h_B} hdh$$

$$q\,x\Big|_0^L = -K\frac{h^2}{2}\Big|_{h_A}^{h_B}$$

$$qL = -K\left(\frac{h_B^2 - h_A^2}{2}\right)$$

$$q = -\frac{1}{2}K\left(\frac{h_B^2 - h_A^2}{L}\right)$$

$$q = \frac{1}{2}K\left(\frac{h_A^2 - h_B^2}{L}\right)$$

Reference: PERH 1.2 Section 6.6.2.1 Darcy's Law

(Answer C)

Aquifers

Problem 22 Solution:

The equation of unconfined aquifer (Dupuit formula):

$$Q = \frac{K\pi\left(h_2^{\,2} - h_1^{\,2}\right)}{\ln\left(\dfrac{r_2}{r_1}\right)}$$

Where:

h_1 and h_2 = depth of water in observation wells 1 and 2 (ft)

r_1 and r_2 = centerline distance from the well and observation wells 1 and 2, respectively (ft)

$h_1 = 45 - 13 = 32$ ft
$h_2 = 45 - 2.45 = 42.55$ ft
$r_1 = 150$ ft
$r_2 = 600$ ft
$K = 0.00788$ ft/s

$$Q = \frac{K\pi\left(h_2^{\,2} - h_1^{\,2}\right)}{\ln\left(\dfrac{r_2}{r_1}\right)}$$

$$Q = \frac{0.00788 \times \pi\left(42.55^2 - 32^2\right)}{\ln\left(\dfrac{600}{150}\right)}$$

$$Q = 14.04 \approx 14 \text{ ft}^3/\text{s}$$

Reference: PERH 1.2 Section 6.6.3.1 Unconfined Aquifers

(Answer D)

Wastewater Flow Rates

Problem 23 Solution:

Computations:

Given: average peaking flow rate = 50,500,500 gpd

peaking factor = 2.4

Find: peak wastewater flow rate

$$\text{peaking factor} = \frac{\text{peak wastewater flow rate}}{\text{average wastewater flow rate}}$$

Transforming the equation to find the peak wastewater flow rate.

$$\text{peak wastewater flow rate} = \text{peaking factor} \times \text{average wastewater flow rate}$$
$$= 2.4 \times 50{,}500{,}500$$
$$= 120{,}000{,}000 \text{ gpd}$$

Reference: TSS 2014

(Answer C)

Note:

I. For this choice, if the student accidentally divides the value of the average by the peak factor, the result is choice (a).
II. For choices (b) and (d), these are just made to confuse the students, no calculation involved.

Digesters

Problem 24 Solution:

The purpose of secondary treatment in wastewater treatment plants is to remove dissolved and suspended organic matter that remains in the wastewater after primary treatment. Secondary treatment is typically performed by biological processes that use microorganisms to break down organic matter. The most common types of secondary treatment processes used are activated sludge, trickling filters, and rotating biological contactors (RBCs).

Therefore, the correct answer is (C) To remove dissolved and suspended organic matter, and the most common types of secondary treatment processes used are activated sludge, trickling filters, and rotating biological contactors. Answer (A) is incorrect because it describes the removal of inorganic matter, not organic matter, and only lists sedimentation and filtration as treatment processes. Answer (B) is incorrect because it describes the removal of organic matter and only lists sedimentation and disinfection as treatment processes. Answer (D) is incorrect because it describes the removal of inorganic matter and lists activated sludge and trickling filters, which are biological processes used to remove organic matter.

Reference: PERH 1.2 Section 6.8 Wastewater Collection and Treatment – but as a theory question, engineering judgment may need to be used

(Answer C)

Disinfection

Problem 25 Solution:

$$\text{Daily consumption} = 275 \text{ MGD} \times 10 \ \frac{\text{mg}}{\text{L}} \times 8.34 \ \frac{\text{lb}}{\text{gal}} = 229.35 \ \frac{\text{lb}}{\text{day}}$$

Since it is greater than 150 lb/day, use one-ton (short) containers

Conversion: 1 ton (short) = 2,000 lb

Solving for the monthly consumption:

Monthly need = 229.35 lb/day × 30 days/month = 6,880.5 lb/month

Using one-ton container:

$$\text{Number of containers} = \frac{6,880.5 \text{ lb}}{2,000 \text{ lb/ton}} = 3.44 \approx 4$$

Reference: PERH 1.2 Section 6.8.5.6 Biotowers/Trickling Filters

(Answer D)

Note: Answer C might be the student's choice if he happened to round it off. 3.44 rounded off equals 3. However, the need is 3.44 which imply 3 tonnes is not enough. So the answer must be 4. The A and B choices are just to confuse the students.

Denitrification

Problem 26 Solution:

$$C_m = 2.47\left(NO_3 - N\right) + 1.53\left(NO_2 - N\right) + 0.87DO$$

Where: C_m = methanol required (mg/L)

$NO_3 - N$ = nitrate nitrogen removal (mg/L)

$NO_2 - N$ = nitrite nitrogen removal (mg/L)

DO = dissolved oxygen removed (mg/L)

Given:

$NO_3 - N = 20$ mg/L
$NO_2 - N = 0.45$ mg/L
$DO = 2.0$ mg/L

$$C_m = 2.47 \times 20 + 1.53 \times 0.45 + 0.87 \times 2.0 = 51.8 \text{ mg/L}$$

Reference: PERH 1.2 Section 6.8.5.3 Methanol Addition

(Answer B)

Solids Handling (Thickening)

Problem 27 Solution:

$$V_1 P_1 = V_2 P_2$$

Given: $V_2 = 18,000 \text{ ft}^3$

$P_1 = 0.8\%$

$P_2 = 5\%$

$$V_1 = \frac{V_2 P_2}{P_1} = \frac{18,000 \times 5\%}{0.8\%} = 112,500 \text{ ft}^3$$

Reference: PERH 1.2 Section 6.8.5.3. Sludge Production

(Answer C)

Solids Handling (Biological Treatment)

Problem 28 Solution:

The only false statement is option A. The rest are true.

Reference: TSS 2014

(Answer A)

Water Quality (BOD)

Problem 29 Solution:

$$BOD_5 = \frac{(D_1 - D_2) - (B_1 - B_2)f}{P} \text{ (mg/L)}$$

Where:

$D_1 = DO$ of dilluted sample immediately after preparation (mg/L)

$D_2 = DO$ of dilluted sample after incubation of $20°C$ (mg/L)

$B_1 = DO$ of seed control before incubation (mg/L)

$B_2 = DO$ of seed control after incubation (mg/L)

f = ratio of seed in dilluted sample to seed in control

P = percent seed in dilluted sample/percent seed in seed control

Given:

$D_1 = 7.86$ mg/L
$D_2 = 2.5$ mg/L
$B_1 = 8.3$ mg/L
$B_2 = 8.0$ mg/L
$P = 1 / 20 = 0.05$
$f = 1 - P = 0.95$

$$BOD_5 = \frac{(7.86 - 2.5) - (8.3 - 8.0)0.95}{0.05} = 101.5 \approx 101 \text{ mg/L}$$

Reference: PERH 1.2 Section 6.7.3 Biochemical Oxygen Demand

(Answer A)

Chemical Oxygen Demand (COD)

Problem 30 Solution:

Chemical oxygen demand (COD) is a measure of the total organic matter in wastewater, based on the amount of oxygen required to chemically oxidize the organic matter using a strong oxidizing agent. The primary factor affecting the COD test results is the presence of reducing agents, which can interfere with the oxidation process and cause artificially low results.

Therefore, the correct answer is (D) COD is a measure of the total organic matter in wastewater, and the primary factor affecting the COD test results is the presence of reducing agents. Answer (A) is incorrect because it describes suspended solids, which are not directly related to COD. Answer (B) is incorrect because COD is a measure of organic matter, not inorganic matter, and pH is not a primary factor affecting COD. Answer (C) is incorrect because the presence of chloride ions may interfere with the measurement of biochemical oxygen demand (BOD), but not COD.

Reference: PERH 1.2 Section 6.7 Water Quality – but as a theory question, engineering judgment may need to be used

(Answer D)

Risk Assessment and Management

Problem 31 Solution:

Reference: PERH 1.2 Section 6.7.8 Risk Calculation

(Answer D)

Indicator Organisms

Problem 32 Solution:

Biological indicator organism:

Total coliform, fecal coliform, heterotrophic plate count, etc.

Reference: WATER 2018

(Answer B)

General Knowledge –BOD, COD, TSS, DO

Problem 33 Solution:

Total suspended solids or TSS is the most common measure of the amount of solids in wastewater effluent. TSS is the measure of all suspended solids in a liquid, typically expressed in mg/L.

Chemical Oxygen Demand (COD) is a measure of the amount of organic matter oxidized by a strong chemical oxidant. COD is used to measure organic matter in commercial, industrial, and municipal wastes that contain compounds toxic to biological life where the BOD_5 test would not work.

Biochemical Oxygen Demand (BOD) is the quantity of dissolved oxygen consumed by microorganisms during the microbial and chemical oxidation of the constituents contained in a wastewater sample during an incubation period at a given temperature.

Dissolved Oxygen (DO) is the amount of oxygen dissolved in water.

Reference: TSS 2014

(Answer B)

Water Treatment (Demands)

Problem 34 Solution:

To solve for the percent reduction, simply subtract the total demand with reduction devices from the total demand without reduction devices. Then, divide the difference by the total demand without reduction devices. The quotient will be multiplied by 100 to express the answer in percent.

Items	Flow in liters/person/day	
	Without reduction devices	With reduction devices
1. Faucet	65	55
2. Shower head	58	35
3. Washing machine	45	30
4. Toilet	125	90
Total	**293**	**210**

$$\% \text{ reduction} = \frac{293 - 210}{293} \times 100\% = 28.3\%$$

(Answer D)

Possible answers:

a.) $\% \text{ reduction} = \dfrac{293 - 210}{210} \times 100\% = 39.5\%$

b.) $\% \text{ reduction} = 293 - 210 = 83\%$

c.) $\% \text{ reduction} = \dfrac{293 - 210}{4} = 20.75\%$

Water Treatment (coagulation and flocculation)

Problem 35 Solution:

The flocculation equation is:

$$G = \sqrt{\frac{P}{\mu V}} \rightarrow P = G^2 \mu V$$

where G is the mean velocity gradient, P is the input power to the fluid, μ is the dynamic viscosity, and V is the volume.

Given: (see unit conversion on PERH 1.2 Section 1.2 Conversion Factors)

G = 45/sec

μ = 0.01 lbf-sec/ft^2

V = 5000 gal = 5000 gal * 0.134 ft^3/gal = 670 ft^3

$$P = G^2 \mu V$$

$$= \left(\left(\frac{45}{sec}\right)^2\right)\left(0.01\frac{\text{lbf-sec}}{\text{ft}^2}\right)(670 \text{ ft}^3)$$

$$= 13,567.5\frac{\text{ft-lbf}}{\text{s}}$$

$$= 13,567.5\frac{\text{ft-lbf}}{\text{s}} \times 1.818 \times 10^{-3}\frac{hp}{\frac{\text{ft-lbf}}{\text{s}}} \quad \text{or} \quad \frac{13,567.5\frac{\text{ft-lbf}}{\text{s}}}{550\frac{\frac{\text{ft-lbf}}{\text{s}}}{hp}}$$

$$= 24.67 \text{ hp}$$

Reference: PERH 1.2 Section 6.9.2.3 Flocculation

(Answer C)

Water Treatment (Sedimentation)

Problem 36 Solution:

To find the surface dimension of the surface of the tank,

$$v_s = \frac{Q}{A_s} \rightarrow A_s = \frac{Q}{v_s}$$

Where : v_s = settling velocity (ft/s)

A_s = surface area (ft²)

Q = flow (ft³/s)

Given:

$$Q = 282 \text{ ft}^3/\text{min} = 4.7 \text{ ft}^3/\text{s}$$

$$v_s = 0.012 \text{ in/s} = 0.001 \text{ ft/s}$$

$$A_s = \frac{4.7 \text{ ft}^3/\text{s}}{0.001 \text{ ft/s}} = 4700 \text{ ft}^2$$

But it is stated in the problem that the length is three times the width:

$$L = 3W$$

$$A = LW = (3W)W = 3W^2$$

$$W = \sqrt{\frac{A}{3}} = \sqrt{\frac{4700}{3}} = 39.58 \text{ ft} \approx 40 \text{ ft}$$

$$L = 3W = 3 \times 40 = 120 \text{ ft}$$

Reference: PERH 1.2 Section 6.8.5.3 Settling and Section 6.9.6 Settling and Sedimentation

(Answer A)

Water Treatment (Filtration)

Problem 37 Solution:

This problem has a lot given but some given values (such as the size and uniformity coefficient of sand) are only placed in order to confuse you. This is just to test how much you understood the main principle that $Q = AV$.

To solve for the nominal filtration rate,

$$\text{filtration rate} = \frac{\text{volume of treated water produced per day}}{\text{total surface area of filter units}}$$
$$= \frac{4,000,000 \text{ ft}^3/\text{day}}{15 \times 16 \text{ ft} \times 32 \text{ ft}}$$
$$= 520.8 \text{ ft/day}$$

Reference: PERH 1.2 Section 6.9.7.2 Media Filtration

(Answer A)

Water Treatment (Disinfection)

Problem 38 Solution:

Breakpoint is a point where chlorine level exceeded the oxidant demand. The breakpoint is best determined by projecting the decreasing and increasing slopes on either side to their point of intersection. Therefore, the dosage is 5 mg/L (see arrow at the breakpoint below). After the dosage of 5 mg/L, it enters the stage of free chlorine residual.

Chlorine Demand Curve

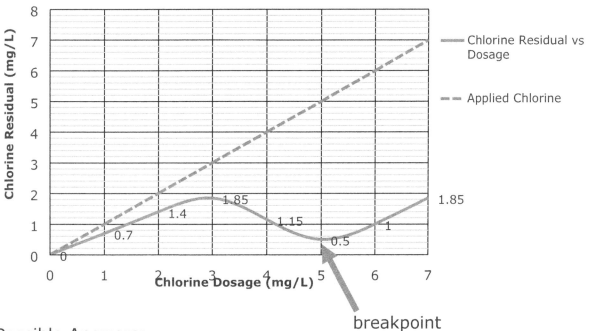

Possible Answers:

a.) **0.5 mg/L** – If the student is careless enough that instead of the dosage, the residual is seen, even though he knows what a breakpoint is, still he might choose this option.

b.) **1.85 mg/L** – If one doesn't understand the term breakpoint, and confused it with the highest numerical value in the curve, 1.85 might be an option. (Not even knowing that 1.85 is the residual, not the dosage) c.) **3 mg/L** – If one doesn't understand the term breakpoint, and confused it with the highest numerical value in the curve, the Chlorine dosage that corresponds to 1.85 mg/L is 3.0 mg/L

d.) **5 mg/L** – correct answer

Reference: TSS 2014
(Answer D)

Water Treatment (General Knowledge)

Problem 39 Solution:

Desalination (also called "desalinization" and "desalting") is the process of removing dissolved salts from water, thus producing fresh water from seawater or brackish water.

Water softening is the removal of calcium, magnesium, and certain other metal cations in hard water.

Water disinfection means the removal, deactivation or killing of pathogenic microorganisms.

Distillation is a process of separating the component substances from a liquid mixture by selective evaporation and condensation.

Reference: WATER 2018

(Answer B)

Engineering Economics (Costing)

Problem 40 Solution:

Solve the work in every motor; consider the 85%-efficiency motor as the first motor, and the 92%-efficiency motor as the second motor. Compute for the work, then the total work, the monthly energy consumption and the cost according to the consumption.

$$\text{Work}_1 = \frac{5 \text{ hp} \times 0.746 \text{ kW/hp}}{0.85} = 4.39 \text{ kW}$$

$$\text{Work}_2 = \frac{5 \text{ hp} \times 0.746 \text{ kW/hp}}{0.92} = 4.05 \text{ kW}$$

$$\text{Total work} = \text{Work}_1 + \text{Work}_2 = 4.39 + 4.05 = 8.44 \text{ kW}$$

$$\text{Monthly use} = 8.44 \text{ kW} \times 24 \text{ hr/day} \times 30 \text{ day/month} = 6{,}079.93 \text{ kW-hr/month}$$

$$\text{Monthly cost} = \frac{\$0.02}{\text{kW-hr}} \times 6{,}07993 \text{ kW-hr} = \$121.60$$

(Answer B)

SCORE SHEET

Correct Answers: _____

Percentage: (correct answers)/40 = _____/40 = _____

Some things to note:

If you can absolutely crush the morning exam then the depth section will be much easier on yourself. You should still shoot for a high score here, but just know if you can get in the upper 90% in the morning then you just need to score more than 20 correct in the afternoon. Imagine if you got all 40 correct in the morning – you'd only need to get 16 right on your depth exam (56/80=70%)! A total of 70% is *about* the passing score for the PE. What's interesting though, is that the depth section will dominate your study time. So, put in the time and practice and you will get there. Keep at it!

LAST SECOND ADVICE AND TIPS

I wanted to wrap up this exam with some tips that I found helpful when I took the exam. Hopefully, they will help you:

1) Make sure you fully understand what your state board and the NCEES requires of you to take the PE exam and to receive your PE. Comply with all rules.

2) You typically need about 3-4 months to really study for the PE. Map out a schedule and study your depth section first. This will allow you to make any adjustments as you get closer to test time. I personally broke down the specification into the 5 major categories of: water resources, transportation, geotechnical, structural, and construction, and spent a couple weeks on each topic with more time devoted to my depth section.

3) Practice everything with the calculator you are going to use on the real exam. You need to become intimately familiar with it.

4) Know where your exam is, where to park, and where you will get food (if you don't plan on bringing your own). Don't be stuck trying to figure this out on test day. You'll regret it.

5) Review courses help. If you can't get motivated, or need the extra help and accountability they offer, then consider taking one. It's worth it to get your PE and get that boost to your career. If you're wondering which one, refer to our helpful tools below.

Helpful Tools:

We have built www.civilengineeringacademy.com to help any civil engineer become a PE. We have tons of free video practice problems there to get you going. We also have plenty of tips, must have resources, advice on courses, and more practice exams that cover your depth section. In addition to this, we have created a civil PE review course that can guide you step-by-step through the entire exam. You can check that out at www.civilpereviewcourse.com.

Made in the USA
Monee, IL
24 April 2023